Oscar Wilde

Quotes...

by The Secret Libraries

Paperback EDITION

Vol.1

Find us on:

The Secret Libraries

Published by The Secret Libraries
www.thesecretlibraries.com
Annotation and Artists Background by The Secret Libraries 2016

Paperback:
ISBN-13: 978-1533211033
ISBN-10: 1533211035

Copyright © 2016

Quotes...

This book provides a selected collection of 204 quotes by Oscar Wilde, the artist's background and further reading.

Oscar Wilde.

1854-1900

Always forgive your enemies; nothing annoys them so much.

Most people are other people. Their thoughts are someone else's opinions, their lives a mimicry, their passions a quotation.

To live is the rarest thing in the world. Most people exist, that is all.

I am so clever that sometimes I don't understand a single word of what I am saying.

We are all in the gutter, but some of us are looking at the stars.

If one cannot enjoy reading a book over and over again, there is no use in reading it at all.

It is what you read when you don't have to that determines what you will be when you can't help it.

The truth is rarely pure and never simple.

The books that the world calls immoral are books that show the world its own shame.

Yes: I am a dreamer. For a dreamer is one who can only find his way by moonlight, and his punishment is that he sees the dawn before the rest of the world.

You can never be overdressed or overeducated.

Be yourself; everyone else is already taken.*

*This quote may have been adapted from "Most people are other people. Their thoughts are someone else's opinions, their lives a mimicry, their passions a quotation.

"

Women are meant to be loved, not to be understood.

"

"

A good friend will always stab you in the front.

"

"

I don't want to go to heaven. None of my friends are there.

"

Never love anyone who treats you like you're ordinary.

Anyone who lives within their means suffers from a lack of imagination.

You will always be fond of me. I represent to you all the sins you never had the courage to commit.

"

Every saint has a past, and every sinner has a future.

"

"

I am not young enough to know everything.

"

"

The heart was made to be broken.

"

You don't love someone for their looks, or their clothes, or for their fancy car, but because they sing a song only you can hear.

"

A thing is not necessarily true because a man dies for it.

"

Experience is merely the name men gave to their mistakes.

Everything in the world is about sex except sex. Sex is about power.

Man is least himself when he talks in his own person. Give him a mask, and he will tell you the truth.

The very essence of romance is uncertainty.

I think God, in creating man, somewhat overestimated his ability.

Those who find ugly meanings in beautiful things are corrupt without being charming. This is a fault. Those who find beautiful meanings in beautiful things are the cultivated. For these there is hope. They are the elect to whom beautiful things mean only Beauty. There is no such thing as a moral or an immoral book. Books are well written, or badly written. That is all.

I never travel without my diary. One should always have something sensational to read in the train.

Death must be so beautiful. To lie in the soft brown earth, with the grasses waving above one's head, and listen to silence. To have no yesterday, and no tomorrow. To forget time, to forgive life, to be at peace.

Some cause happiness wherever they go; others whenever they go.

With freedom, books, flowers, and the moon, who could not be happy?

Education is an admirable thing, but it is well to remember from time to time that nothing that is worth knowing can be taught.

I can resist anything except temptation.

A cynic is a man who knows the price of everything, and the value of nothing.

I don't want to be at the mercy of my emotions. I want to use them, to enjoy them, and to dominate them.

"

To define is to limit.

„

All women become like their mothers. That is their tragedy. No man does, and that is his.

Quotation is a serviceable substitute for wit.

It is absurd to divide people into good and bad. People are either charming or tedious.

The only way to get rid of temptation is to yield to it.

"

Who, being loved, is poor?

"

To love oneself is the beginning of a lifelong romance.

Crying is for plain women. Pretty women go shopping.

Most modern calendars mar the sweet simplicity of our lives by reminding us that each day that passes is the anniversary of some perfectly uninteresting event.

I have the simplest tastes. I am always satisfied with the best.

There is only one thing in the world worse than being talked about, and that is not being talked about.

Selfishness is not living as one wishes to live, it is asking others to live as one wishes to live.

I have nothing to declare except my genius.

Fashion is a form of ugliness so intolerable that we have to alter it every six months.

I am too fond of reading books to care to write them.

A man's face is his autobiography. A woman's face is her work of fiction.

After a good dinner one can forgive anybody, even one's own relations.

No good deed goes unpunished.

Sometimes ascribed to Clare Boothe Luce, The Yale Book of Quotations notes, there is an earlier occurrence of "No good deed goes unpunished" in the Zanesville (Ohio) Signal, November 5, 1942, attributed to Walter Winchell.

Anybody can sympathise with the sufferings of a friend, but it requires a very fine nature to sympathise with a friend's success.

Whenever people agree with me I always feel I must be wrong.

We are each our own devil, and we make this world our hell.

Life is far too important a thing ever to talk seriously about.

When one is in love, one always begins by deceiving one's self, and one always ends by deceiving others. That is what the world calls a romance.

Behind every exquisite thing that existed, there was something tragic.

Children begin by loving their parents; as they grow older they judge them; sometimes they forgive them.

Morality is simply the attitude we adopt towards people we personally dislike.

To lose one parent may be regarded as a misfortune; to lose both looks like carelessness.

Every woman is a rebel.

"

Only dull people are brilliant at breakfast.

"

I like men who have a future and women who have a past.

"

The world is a stage and the play is badly cast.

"

Never marry at all, Dorian. Men marry because they are tired, women, because they are curious: both are disappointed.

To get back my youth I would do anything in the world, except take exercise, get up early, or be respectable.

I choose my friends for their good looks, my acquaintances for their good characters, and my enemies for their good intellects.

Art is the only serious thing in the world. And the artist is the only person who is never serious.

We live in an age when unnecessary things are our only necessities.

A bore is someone who deprives you of solitude without providing you with company.

How can a woman be expected to be happy with a man who insists on treating her as if she were a perfectly normal human being.

If you are not long, I will wait for you all my life.

There are only two kinds of people who are really fascinating: people who know absolutely everything, and people who know absolutely nothing.

Humanity takes itself too seriously. It is the world's original sin. If the cave-man had known how to laugh, History would have been different.

The suspense is terrible. I hope it will last.

Nowadays most people die of a sort of creeping common sense, and discover when it is too late that the only things one never regrets are one's mistakes.

America is the only country that went from barbarism to decadence without civilization in between.

Everything in moderation, including moderation.

Nothing can cure the soul but the senses, just as nothing can cure the senses but the soul.

There are moments when one has to choose between living one's own life, fully, entirely, completely-or dragging out some false, shallow, degrading existence that the world in its hypocrisy demands.

Society often forgives the criminal; it never forgives the dreamer.

Words! Mere words! How terrible they were!

How clear, and vivid, and cruel! One could not escape from them. And yet what a subtle magic there was in them! They seemed to be able to give a plastic form to formless things, and to have a music of their own as sweet as that of viol or of lute. Mere words! Was there anything so real as words?

Live! Live the wonderful life that is in you! Let nothing be lost upon you. Be always searching for new sensations. Be afraid of nothing.

"

There is no sin except stupidity.

"

The public have an insatiable curiosity to know everything, except what is worth knowing.

Some things are more precious because they don't last long.

Art finds her own perfection within, and not outside of herself. She is not to be judged by any external standard of resemblance. She is a veil, rather than a mirror.

Paradoxically though it may seem, it is none the less true that life imitates art far more than art imitates life.

An idea that is not dangerous is unworthy of being called an idea at all.

Indeed I have always been of the opinion that hard work is simply the refuge of people who have nothing to do.

I may not agree with you, but I will defend to the death your right to make an ass of yourself.

"

The nicest feeling in the world is to do a good deed anonymously-and have somebody find out.

"

One should never trust a woman who tells one her real age. A woman who would tell one that would tell one anything.

Women have a much better time than men in this world; there are far more things forbidden to them.

Life is too short to learn German.

Laughter is not at all a bad beginning for a friendship, and it is by far the best ending for one.

I always pass on good advice. It is the only thing to do with it. It is never of any use to oneself.

The good ended happily, and the bad unhappily. That is what Fiction means.

Every portrait that is painted with feeling is a portrait of the artist, not of the sitter.

There are many things that we would throw away if we were not afraid that others might pick them up.

The world is changed because you are made of ivory and gold. The curves of your lips rewrite history.

There is no such thing as a moral or an immoral book. Books are well written, or badly written. That is all.

Whenever a man does a thoroughly stupid thing, it is always from the noblest motives.

It takes great deal of courage to see the world in all its tainted glory, and still to love it.

A little sincerity is a dangerous thing, and a great deal of it is absolutely fatal.

They've promised that dreams can come true - but forgot to mention that nightmares are dreams, too.

You can help me. You can open for me the portals of death's house, for love is always with you, and love is stronger than death is.

You must have a cigarette. A cigarette is the perfect type of a perfect pleasure. It is exquisite, and it leaves one unsatisfied. What more can one want?

The public is wonderfully tolerant. It forgives everything except genius.

I have grown to love secrecy. It seems to be the one thing that can make modern life mysterious or marvelous to us. The commonest thing is delightful if only one hides it.

In this world there are only two tragedies. One is not getting what one wants, and the other is getting it.

The basis of optimism is sheer terror.

Hear no evil, speak no evil, and you won't be invited to cocktail parties.

This wallpaper is dreadful, one of us will have to go.

The mystery of love is greater than the mystery of death.

I never put off till tomorrow what I can possibly do - the day after.

Music makes one feel so romantic - at least it always gets on one's nerves - which is the same thing nowadays.

He has no enemies, but is intensely disliked by his friends.

One should always be in love. That's the reason one should never marry.

I like persons better than principles, and I like persons with no principles better than anything else in the world.

Only the shallow know themselves.

Keep love in your heart. A life without it is like a sunless garden when the flowers are dead. The consciousness of loving and being loved brings a warmth and a richness to life that nothing else can bring.

"

All art is quite useless.

"

132

A man can be happy with any woman as long as he
does not love her.

Because to influence a person is to give him one's own soul. He does not think his natural thoughts, or burn with his natural passions. His virtues are not real to him. His sins, if there are such things as sins, are borrowed. He becomes an echo of some one else's music, an actor of a part that has not been written for him.

The world was my oyster but I used the wrong fork.

Life is never fair, and perhaps it is a good thing for most of us that it is not.

She is all the great heroines of the world in one. She is more than an individual. I love her, and I must make her love me. I want to make Romeo jealous. I want the dead lovers of the world to hear our laughter, and grow sad. I want a breath of our passion to stir dust into consciousness, to wake their ashes into pain.

The aim of life is self-development. To realize one's nature perfectly - that is what each of us is here for.

Disobedience, in the eyes of any one who has read history, is man's original virtue. It is through disobedience that progress has been made, through disobedience and through rebellion.

Consistency is the hallmark of the unimaginative.

The most terrible thing about it is not that it breaks one's heart—hearts are made to be broken—but that it turns one's heart to stone.

Always! That is a dreadful word. It makes me shudder when I hear it. Women are so fond of using it. They spoil every romance by trying to make it last forever. It is a meaningless word, too. The only difference between a caprice and a life-long passion is that the caprice lasts a little longer.

She is very clever, too clever for a woman. She lacks the indefinable charm of weakness.

I love acting. It is so much more real than life.

I don't like compliments, and I don't see why a man should think he is pleasing a woman enormously when he says to her a whole heap of things that he doesn't mean.

I won't tell you that the world matters nothing, or the world's voice, or the voice of society. They matter a good deal. They matter far too much. But there are moments when one has to choose between living one's own life, fully, entirely, completely—or dragging out some false, shallow, degrading existence that the world in its hypocrisy demands. You have that moment now. Choose!

I hope you have not been leading a double life, pretending to be wicked and being good all the time. That would be hypocrisy.

Everything popular is wrong.

She behaves as if she was beautiful. Most American women do. It is the secret of their charm.

If I am occasionally a little over-dressed, I make up for it by being always immensely over-educated.

Life has been your art. You have set yourself to music. Your days are your sonnets.

The one charm about the past is that it is the past.

I am tired of myself tonight. I should like to be somebody else.

No man is rich enough to buy back his past.

We women, as some one says, love with our ears, just as you men love with your eyes...

*From the novel The Picture of Dorian Gray.

One can always be kind to people about whom one cares nothing.

Between men and women there is no friendship possible. There is passion, enmity, worship, love, but no friendship.

I knew nothing but shadows and I thought them to be real.

You like every one; that is to say, you are indifferent to every one.

Punctuality is the thief of time.

One should always play fairly when one has the winning cards.

Illusion is the first of all pleasures.

Work is the curse of the drinking classes.

Irony is wasted on the stupid.

It is only shallow people who do not judge by appearances. The true mystery of the world is the visible, not the invisible....

Friendship is far more tragic than love. It lasts longer.

There is a luxury in self-reproach. When we blame ourselves, we feel that no one else has a right to blame us. It is the confession, not the priest, that gives us absolution.

One has a right to judge a man by the effect he has over his friends.

In old days books were written by men of letters and read by the public. Nowadays books are written by the public and read by nobody.

Ah! The strength of women comes from the fact that psychology cannot explain us. Men can be analyzed, women...merely adored.

A man who does not think for himself does not think at all.

I adore simple pleasures. They are the last refuge of the complex.

When the Gods wish to punish us, they answer our prayers.

When a woman marries again, it is because she detested her first husband. When a man marries again, it is because he adored his first wife. Women try their luck; men risk theirs.

After the first glass, you see things as you wish they were. After the second, you see things as they are not. Finally, you see things as they really are, and that is the most horrible thing in the world.

Ordinary riches can be stolen, real riches cannot. In your soul are infinitely precious things that cannot be taken from you.

Misfortunes one can endure--they come from outside, they are accidents. But to suffer for one's own faults--ah!--there is the sting of life.

Life is not complex. We are complex. Life is simple, and the simple thing is the right thing.

The reason we all like to think so well of others is that we are all afraid for ourselves.

Hearts live by being wounded.

He is really not so ugly after all, provided, of course, that one shuts one's eyes, and does not look at him.

I love to talk about nothing. It's the only thing I know anything about.

I hate people who are not serious about meals. It is so shallow of them.

Popularity is the one insult I have never suffered.

"

In matters of grave importance, style, not sincerity, is the vital thing.

"

I really don't see anything romantic in proposing. It is very romantic to be in love. But there is nothing romantic about a definite proposal. Why, one may be accepted. One usually is, I believe. Then the excitement is all over. The very essence of romance is uncertainty. If ever I get married, I'll certainly try to forget the fact.

Wickedness is a myth invented by good people to account for the curious attractiveness of others.

I was working on the proof of one of my poems all the morning, and took out a comma. In the afternoon I put it back again.

I have no objection to anyone's sex life as long as they don't practice it in the street and frighten the horses.

A pessimist is somebody who complains about the noise when opportunity knocks.

It takes great courage to see the world in all its tainted glory, and still to love it. And even more courage to see it in the one you love.

My own business always bores me to death; I prefer other people's.

"

Conformity is the last refuge of the unimaginitive.

"

Experience is one thing you can't get for nothing.

As long as a woman can look ten years younger than her daughter, she is perfectly satisfied.

People who count their chickens before they are hatched act very wisely because chickens run about so absurdly that it's impossible to count them accurately.

They get up early, because they have so much to do, and go to bed early, because they have so little to think about.

I never change, except in my affections.

Nothing that is worth knowing can be taught.

Memory is the diary we all carry about with us.

"

How else but through a broken heart may Lord Christ enter in?

"

There was so much in you that charmed me that I felt I must tell you something about yourself. I thought how tragic it would be if you were wasted.

Never speak disrespectfully of Society, Algernon. Only people who can't get into it do that.

It is the stupid and the ugly who have the best of it in this world.

Sin is a thing that writes itself across a man's face. It cannot be concealed.

Ultimately the bond of all companionship, whether in marriage or in friendship, is conversation, and conversation must have a common basis, and between two people of widely different culture the only common basis possible is the lowest level.

It is only shallow people who require years to get rid of an emotion. A man who is master of himself can end a sorrow as easily as he can invent a pleasure. I don't want to be at the mercy of my emotions. I want to use them, to enjoy them, and to dominate them.

There is always something ridiculous about the emotions of people whom one has ceased to love.

I see when men love women. They give them but a little of their lives. But women when they love give everything.

Oscar Wilde

1854-1900

Artists Background

On the 16th of October 1854 Oscar Fingal O'Flahertie Wills Wilde was born, at 21 Westland Row, Dublin, Ireland. He was a poet, critic, playwright, author and a celebrity in late 19th century (Victorian era) London. After writing in diverse forms throughout the 1880s, he became one of London's most popular playwrights in the early 1890s. He is best known for his novel 'The Picture of Dorian Gray' (first published in July 1890) and the play 'The Importance of Being Earnest' (1895), as well as his wit and the circumstances of his arrest and imprisonment leading to an early death.

Oscar Wilde had two brothers (Willie and Henry) and two sisters (Isola and Emily). His mother Jane Francesca Wilde (1821-1896) was a poet and literary hostess, his father Sir William Wilde (1815-1876) a successful surgeon. Wilde was first educated at the Portora Royal School at Enniskillen and then the Trinity College in Dublin (1871- 1874) wining a scholarship by competitive examination in his second year and the Berkeley Gold Medal in his final year. He went on to win a Demyship scholarship to study at the Magdalen College, Oxford. After graduation from Oxford, he moved to London and published his first collection of poetry 'Poems' (1881). In 1882, Wilde travelled to New York City to give an American lecture tour. He married a wealthy Englishwoman, Constance Mary Lloyd (1858-1898) in 1884 and they had two sons Cyril (1885-1915) and Vyvyan (1886-1967). In 1886 Oscar Wilde was hired to run the magazine Lady's World, shortly after he started a seven-year period of creativity in 1888, during which he produced nearly all of his great literary works.

In 1891 Wilde began an affair with Lord Alfred Douglas, nicknamed 'Bosie'. Oscar Wilde sued Bosie's father, the Marquis of Queensberry for libel, whilst his masterpiece the comedy 'The Importance of Being Earnest' (1895) was still on stage in London. The trial unearthed evidence that caused him to drop his charges and led to his own arrest and trial for gross indecency with men under Section 11 of the Criminal Law Amendment Act 1885 (The acquittal left him bankrupt as Wilde was legally liable for the considerable expenses the Marquis of Queensberry had incurred). After a further two trials Oscar Wilde was convicted and sentenced to two years hard labour. He entered prison on the 25th May 1895.

In 1897 whilst still in prison, he wrote a long letter to Bossie published posthumously under the title of De Profundis in 1905. His wife took their children to Switzerland and adopted the name 'Holland'. Oscar Wilde was released on the 18th May 1897 and travelled to Dieppe, France. Wilde's health was greatly damaged from the time spent in prison. He spent his last three years in impoverished exile (He never returned to Ireland or Britain). During this time he took the name of "Sebastian Melmoth". On the 25th of November Oscar Wilde had developed cerebral meningitis. He died on the 30th of November 1900 in Paris, France, destitute at the age of 46.

References & Further Reading
Works from Oscar Wilde

Novels:
The Picture of Dorian Gray

Essays:
The Decay of Lying
The Soul of Man under Socialism
The Critic as Artist"
De Profundis

Short stories:
The Canterville Ghost
The Portrait of Mr. W. H.

Collections:
Lord Arthur Savile's Crime and Other Stories
The Happy Prince and Other Stories
A House of Pomegranates

Plays:
Vera; or, The Nihilists
The Duchess of Padua
Lady Windermere's Fan
A Florentine Tragedy
A Woman of No Importance
Salome
La Sainte Courtisane
An Ideal Husband
The Importance of Being Earnest

oscar Wilde.

Quotes...

Receive a Kindle Edition in the series for FREE...

Sign up at
www.theSecretlibraries.com

Find us on:

The Secret Libraries

Published by The Secret Libraries
www.thesecretlibraries.com
Annotation and Artists Background by The Secret Libraries 2016

Paperback:
ISBN-13: 978-1533211033
ISBN-10: 1533211035

For more information please find us at:

www.the secret libraries.com

Thank you for your purchase.

Printed in Great Britain
by Amazon